너를 맞아 보낸다
Sending you after meeting you
2

정송전 한영시집
Korean-English Poems Collection of Jeong Song Jeon

을지출판공사

■ 자서自序

　삶의 다양한 모습과 고단한 숨결이 시의 눈을 틔우고 오만 가지 허드레 잡념까지도 내게로 와서 시가 되었을 때, 그것은 돌올한 내 시의 성취라면 성취라고 감히 자부한다.
　나는 내 시집 〈내 이렇게 살다가〉의 자서에 다음과 같이 적은 적이 있다.
　'나의 여정은 분명 저녁나절쯤이지만 나의 시는 아직 새벽이다. 그래서 하염없이 회안에 젖는다.'
　내 삶이 어느 날 느닷없이 내가 아닌 것처럼 비춰지기도 했으며 삶의 질곡이 부질없이 그리움으로 다가오기도 했음을 고백한다. 그러나 그럴 때마다 내 삶의 심지를 곧추세우는 의연한 '여유'가 나를 건져 내기도 했다. 이것이 내 시의 이력이자 본령이라는 것을 나는 잊지 않는다.
　끝으로, 이 영문시집 펴내는데 있어 아내(신미자)와 아들(정주헌) 노고가 컸음을 밝혀 둔다.

2022. 5. 10

지은이 정송전

The Preface of the Poet

When the various aspects and the weary breath of life put forth a bud of poetry and even tens of thousands of miscellaneous trivia thoughts come to me and become poetry, if I can call it, I dare to say that's the accomplishment of my outstanding poetry.

I once wrote the following in my essay for my collection of poems, 〈Living like this〉.

'My journey is certainly about the evening, but my poem is still dawn. So, I get soaked in endless remorse.'

I confess that one day my life suddenly felt like it wasn't me, and that life's ordeal came to me in vain longing. But every time that happened, the resolute 'Composure' that made my life upright, saved me. I do not forget that this is the history and the original characteristic of my poetry.

To conclude, I would like to acknowledge the efforts of my wife (Mija Shin) and son (Jooheon Jeong) in writing this English poem collection.

2022. 5. 10

Author Jeong Song jeon

차례

- 자서自序 The Preface of the Poet · 2
- 저자 약력 · 156

제1부 삶의 고단함이 펼치는 그리움의 난장
Part 1 The Chaos of Longing that the Rigors of Life Unfold

꽃과 섬 A flower and an island / 10
떠서사는 구름이 The floating cloud is / 14
고향 길 My hometown road / 18
섬 사람 · 2 An islander · 2 / 20
양지동 소묘 · 5 Yangji-dong sketch · 5 / 22
삶의 한가운데 서서 Standing in the middle of life / 24
밤 호수 별 Night Lake Star / 26
사랑의 여백 The space of love / 28
잊혀짐에 대하여 Regarding oblivion / 30
돌아오지 않는 것을 위하여 For the things that never returned / 32
떠난 길 The road that is left / 36
꽃상여 A funeral bier decorated with flowers / 38
나의 평행선 My parallel line / 42
나를 정리하며 Organizing me / 44
기대期待 The expectation / 46

Table of ontents

제 2 부 이별의 뒤란에서 만남의 뜨락으로
Part 2   From the Back of Farewell to the Garden of a Meeting

꿈 The dream / 52

이별 뒤 After farewell / 54

만남으로 With a meeting / 56

바람 엽서 A windy postcard / 60

바람의 말 · 1 A word of the winds · 1 / 62

진달래꽃 An Azalea Flower / 64

외 출 Going out / 68

섬을 떠나는 바다 The sea, leaving the island / 70

여정에서 On the journey / 72

바람의 침묵 · 3 The silence of the wind · 3 / 76

하늘은 적막을 더한다 The sky increases silence / 78

안 부 · 2 Best regards · 2 / 80

지난 봄날에 Last spring / 82

너를 맞아 보낸다 Sending you after meeting you / 84

꽃과 바람 A flower and the wind / 86

차례

제3부 안부의 문턱에서 기도의 모서리로
Part 3 From the Threshold of the Best Regards to the Corner of the Prayer

당신의 일상日常 Your daily life / 90
기도에 대하여 About prayer / 92
알 수 없는 마음 Unknown mind / 94
환幻 Unreality / 96
어떤 전율 Certain trembles / 98
산 속에서 In the mountains / 100
오늘도 Today again / 102
헌 책방에서 At the used book store / 104
돌아보는 밀어 The secret word that is looking back / 106
가을 문턱 The threshold of autumn / 108
밤의 정경 The landscape of the night / 110
그림자가 머무는 곳에 Where the shadow stays / 112
소식을 마중하며 Greeting the news / 114
그믐밤에 On the last night of a lunar month / 118

Table of ontents

제4부 기다림의 반석에는 사랑의 되새김이
Part 4 On the Foundation of Waiting, the Reflection of Love is

답신答信 A reply / 122

바람이었지 It was a wind / 124

정 적 Stillness / 126

가 뭄 The drought / 128

그림자의 흔적 The trace of a shadow / 130

안면도 할매섬 Grandma Island, Anmyeondo / 132

빗속의 밤차 The night train in the rain / 134

너와 나는 You and I / 136

오늘도 나는 Today I also / 138

숲 속의 가로등 The street lamp in the forest / 140

그대 사는 것 What you live / 142

헛소리 중에서 Among nonsense / 144

지금 나는 Now I am / 146

오늘 그리고 내일 Today and tomorrow / 150

채색된 여운으로 As a lingering imagery / 154

제1부 Part 1

삶의 고단함이 펼치는 그리움의 난장
The Chaos of Longing that the Rigors of Life Unfold

아직도 미지의 한 켠에
끓어오름으로 우두커니 서서
떠날 줄 모르는 얼굴.

저승으로 지고 갈
너무나 작고 초라한 나를
하늘 빈자리에 남겨두면 어떤가.
- 「나를 정리하며」 중에서

Still in one corner of the unknown,
Standing around boilingly
The face that cannot leave.

Will carry it on my back to the afterlife
So small and humble me
How about leaving it in the spare place of the sky?
- The part of 「Organizing me」

꽃과 섬

소금기 배인 안개가 갈매기 깃에 너울거린다.
뱃고동은 감각으로 풍상을 휘젓는다.

바람은 마음 삭히는 눈빛이지만
신기루같은 섬이 있어
파도는 분수없이 설레인다.

하늘이 화폭에 내려 앉는다.
사무치던 세월
무슨 수로 풀어서
뱃길에 하얀 물보라 되었는가.
가득한 눈물로 떠난 모습
머리맡에 가즈런히 앉혀 놓고
푸르디푸른 그리움을 고르는가.

하늘이 비에 젖는다.
파란 행복을 정박시킨다.

A flower and an island

The fog with saltness sways by the seagull feathers.
The foghorn is flapping the wind and frost with its senses.

The wind has a glance that smooths its mind but
There is an island like a mirage,
The waves flutter unwisely.

The sky is descending on the canvas.
The poignant years
How could it solve and
Become a white spray on a seaway?
Leaving with full tears
Seating it neatly on the head side,
Does it choose the bluest longing?

The sky is wet with rain,
Anchors blue happiness.

숨겨도 숨겨도 뉘엿대는 별들 곁에서
그득한 봄햇살로 꺾어
촉감으로 물드는 너는
항상 풋풋하거라.

나는 섬으로 앉아 있으면서도
꽃 속의 떨림으로
또 한 번 무릎을 꿇는다.

Near stars that are ready to sink despite being hidden and hidden,
Broken by full spring sunshine
Colored with tactility, you
Be fresh always.

I am sitting as even an island
By the tremor inside a flower
Once again, I kneel down.

떠서 사는 구름이

살구나무 밑둥에 진이 흘러 고인
진딧물의 무덤 속으로
영세의 개미들이 줄지어 간다.

사랑을 됫박으로 퍼낸다고
누가 탓하랴만
진동하는 항구의 비린내여,
너의 가슴을 오려 오면서
시절은 기가 꺾인다.

퍼렇게 매어달린 살구 속으로
입덧의 햇살이 포개지만
귓속의 창들이 열린다.

밤이면 가지런한 세포들이
활기차게 생동하는 동안
사방에 가뭄 탄
바람이 서 있다.

The floating cloud is

The sap flows, pooled under the apricot tree
Into the tomb of aphids
The petty ants line up.

Scooping up love with a gourd bowl
Who could blame it?
The full fishy odor of harbor,
Cutting your heart
The years are discouraged.

Into the apricot hanging blue
The sunshine of morning sickness is folded but
The windows of the inner ear open.

At night, while neat cells,
Are lively living
Everywhere burned from drought
The wind is standing.

밤이 되면 빛이래
별빛뿐인 고향 산자락을 돌아
뭉개버린 꿈을
맨몸으로 풍요롭게 하는
정녕 바람이기에.

At night, the light is merely
Just starlight, there, turning around the hillside of hometown
The crushed dream
Flourishing it with a bare body,
Because it's really the wind.

고향 길

고향으로 가는 길은
한밤중도 이미 깨어 있다.
둥둥 떠 있는 어릴적 구름과 산
그 길에 아직도 고향은 깨어 있다.
고향으로 가는 시골길은
문명을 앞서가고 있다.
고향으로 가는 시골길에서
만나는 장승의
흐릿한 형상은
긴 세월을 살아온 소박함이여
넘쳐흐르는 풍습으로
내일을 바라본다.
고향으로 가는 시골길은
저마다 봄동산 나들이다.

My hometown road

On way hometown
Midnight is already awake.
Floating clouds and the mountain of childhood
On that road, my hometown is still awake.
The country road to hometown is
Ahead of civilization.
On the country road to hometown
Met with the totem pole
Its vague shape is,
The simplicity that had lived for long years
With overflowing custom,
Looking to the future.
On the country road to hometown
Each one is the outing of spring hills.

섬 사람 · 2

바다도
하늘도
온통 푸르다.

바다가
하늘이
온통 비었다.

바다에 하늘이
하늘에 바다가 겹쳐
온통 쪽빛으로 파닥인다.

거기 사람 하나 둘
모여 살며
정을 사귀어 나눈다.

An islander · 2

The sea and
The sky also
All are blue.

The sea and
The sky
All are empty.

The sky over the sea
Are overlapped with the sea under the sky
All are fluttering with indigo blue.

One or two persons
Are living together,
Get along and share with affections.

양지동 소묘 · 5

슬픈 소꿉놀이었지
손때 묻은 세간이래야
몽그라진 부지깽이
하얀 소금 몇 움큼의
아린 추억.

60년대에는
시詩도
도깨비도
형제였었지.

Yangji-dong sketch · 5

It was a sad play at housekeeping
Household goods with hand-stained are
A crumbled wooden poker
Handfuls of white salts
The aching recollection.

In the sixties
The poems and
A goblin also,
Were brothers.

삶의 한가운데 서서

철이 든 만큼 마음이 여려짐은
안개를 말아 올린 바람 때문일까.
흙탕물을 들이마신 역겨움 때문일까.

사방의 시선을 불러내어
삶의 모닥불을 뒤척인다.
내 영혼에 불을 밝히는 이
그래, 전생으로 가자.

비록 너의 기억에 지워진
생시의 한가운데 주저앉아
걸어잠근 문고리.

공간이 없는 시간 속으로
속박을 풀어놓는다.
시간이 다시 살아난다.

흔들리는 어둠을 일깨워
가로등이 발화점 되어
그림자는 빈 집 뜰에 가득하기만 하다.

Standing in the middle of life

My mind is fragile as much as matured,
Is it because of the wind that rolled up the fog?
Is it because of the disgust of drinking muddy water?

Evoking the gaze of everywhere
Stirring the bonfire of life.
The one who lights up my soul
Right, Let's go to the prior life.

Even if it's erased from your memory,
In the middle of reality, sat down
The locked doorknob.

Into the time without space
Unfastening restraint.
Time is being resurrected.

Awakening the shaking darkness
The street lamp becomes the ignition point and
The shadows just fill the empty house yard.

밤 호수 별

밤이 잠든 호수에
별들이 내려앉는다.

별들의 숨소리가
안개로 피어 오르고

넘쳐나는 적막 가운데
하늘은 그대로다.

어둠 속의 형상은
매만져 더듬어 볼수록
아득히 떠오르다 번진다.

가까이 스쳐가는 소리결
우주 한가운데 길
내 길이 보인다.

Night Lake Star

On the lake where night sleeps
The stars are descending.

The breath sounds of the stars,
Are blooming into the mist.

In the middle of overflowing silence
The sky is as it is.

The shape in the dark
As trimming and groping it,
It emerges and disperses afar.

The layer of sound that is closely sweeping
The road in the middle of the universe
I see my road.

사랑의 여백

창세기와 희랍에 최초의 여자는
이브와 판도라.

이들은
다같이 계율을 어기고
다같이 사랑을 갈구했다.

잉태의 고통과 유혹의 호기심으로
감성은 가랑잎이 되어

이제도 누군가를 사랑하고 있는
경건함이여.

되돌릴 수 없는 세월이며
예감에 물든 하늘도
바람 젖어 서럽다.

The space of love

The first woman in the Genesis and Greece
Eve and Pandora.

They
All together violate the commandments
All together yearn for love.

With the pain of pregnancy and the curiosity of temptation
Sensibility becomes fallen leaves and

Still loving someone
That piety, it is.

Irreversible time and
The sky is dyed by premonition also,
Get sad by windy wetness.

잊혀짐에 대하여

단념하고 한 세상 살아왔는데
가을 바람이 가슴 속을 휑덩 스치고 가더니
화들짝 꽃맘으로 피어남은 왜일까.
아, 지친 일신의 순수 그대로
불꽃으로 사그라지는 잊혀짐이 왜일까.

Regarding oblivion

Have lived in a world with my abandonment
The autumn winds have swept through my heart and
Why does it startlingly bloom into the flower mind?
Ah, the purity of the exhausted body, as it is
Why is the oblivion diminishing as flames?

돌아오지 않는 것을 위하여

달빛에 씻긴 바람이
멀리 떠나려 한다.
꽃 그늘이
바람의 길을 막고 서 있다.

속절없는 게
어디 세월뿐이랴.

마주보고 앉아 있어도
내 깨닫지 못하는 거리감
무슨 수로 눈에 들게 하겠는가.

잠든 사이에 자신을 모두 숨길 수만 있다면
세상의 얼룩을 지워주고 싶다.

하룻내 손길을 부비는 것은
잘못을 비는 바람의 사역이다.

For the things that never returned

The wind washed away by the moonlight,
Tries to leave afar.
The shade of flower,
Stands against the windy road.

The inevitable thing,
Aren't the years the only thing?

Even sitting face to face
The distance that I can't realize,
How can I catch its fancy?

If I could hide all of myself during sleeping
I want to erase all the worldly stains.

Rubbing hands all day long is
The religious duty of the winds for apologizing faults.

바람을 찾아 나선다.
가고 오지 않는 것이 없다면
기다림이 무슨 소용인가.

돌아오지 않는 것을 위하여
속박 속으로 나를 몰아 넣는다.

I come out to seek the wind.
If nothing goes and returns
What's the use of waiting?

For the things that never returned,
I drive me into the restraint.

떠난 길

푸르름만 움켜 쥐고
그 떠난 길
꿈이라 할까.

안개 속의 햇살처럼
소복한 아낙은
맨발로 내달리며 생바람이 된다.

혼자 뜨락에서
꽃잎 오무리는 꽃대궁을 본다.
삶처럼 지평은
저리도 허망한 순수인 것을
어찌 꿈이라고만 할까.

이슬 속의 하늘을
가지런히 눕혀 놓고
다시 만날 수 없는 눈짓에
푸르름으로 떠난다.

The road that is left

Grasping only the blueness
That road he left
Could it call as the dream?

Like the sunshine in the mist
Woman wearing white mourning clothes,
Become a fresh wind running with bare feet.

Alone in the yard
Seeing the flower stalk that puckers its petals.
The horizon like life
That's so vain purity
How could it be called just the dream?

The sky in the dew
Laying it down trimly
In a glance which can never meet again
Leaving as a bluish thing.

꽃상여

숲 속으로 길을 내며
꽃상여가
소복의 아낙을 허공에 떠올린다.

요령은 하늘을 넓히고
만장은 갈잎으로 히덕거리며
무슨 말을 씌워주랴.

아득함 가까이
비로소 빈 산천이 아늑하다.

지내온 날과 달은
황량한 숲 속을
어디쯤 비켜가고 있을까.

요령 소리결
하늘 밖으로 내달리는 바람 가둬
끌어안아 덮어준다.

A funeral bier decorated with flowers

Making way into the forest
A funeral bier decorated with flowers,
Rising a woman in white mourning clothes in the air.

The funeral bell is to widen the sky
The funeral streamers keep boisterous with oak leaves.
What words shall be written on it?

Farness is close
Finally, the empty mountain and river are cozy.

The days and months that have passed through
In the desolate forest
Whereabouts are they passing aside?

With the sound of the funeral bell
Traps the wind that is running outward the sky,
Embraces and covers it.

다시금 꿈이 있을 거야
너울에 씻겨 온
그윽한 꿈이 있을 거야.
두 팔을 휘젓는 몸짓으로
시름자락 들추어 일어서는 아낙이여.

There will be a dream again

Being washed by surging waves,

It must be a profound dream.

With a gesture of stirring her arms,

The woman, who stands up with lifting the skirt of grief.

나의 평행선

완행열차가 지친 모습으로
산 언덕을 달린다.

우울한 날이면 나도
같은 길을 따라 나선다.

마주한 얼굴빛은 환하다가
속으론 바위등 돌리며
마냥 서성거리겠지.

이제 나의 비유는 끝나고
무너질 말을
새길 일만 남았는가.

나의 평행선은
언제나 갈래길이면서
끝나질 않는다.

My parallel line

The slow train with a weary appearance,
Runs on the mountain hills.

On a gloomy day I also,
Follow the same road.

The faced complexion becomes bright
Underneath it, with turning the back of rock and
Will hang around all the time.

Now my metaphor is over
The corroding words
Will I only need to carve it?

My parallel line is
Always a fork in the road and
An endless one.

나를 정리하며

버리지 못하는 허물
담아 놓고 다시 덜어내어
입김으로 촉촉이 적시거나
다시 햇살에 말리며
알 수 없는 짓으로
나를 괴롭혀도
구름은 그저 유영할 뿐이다.

아직도 미지의 한 켠에
끓어오름으로 우두커니 서서
떠날 줄 모르는 얼굴.

저승으로 지고 갈
너무나 작고 초라한 나를
하늘 빈자리에 남겨두면 어떤가.

언제나 풋풋한 그 하늘
세월마저 안가고 맴돌면 어쩌나
지친 마음에
나뭇가지의 흔들림을 자기 탓으로 알면 어쩌나.

Organizing me

My fault that cannot be thrown away
Put it in and take it out again
Moisturizing wetly by the breath or
Dry it again with sunshine
By doing inexplicably,
Harass me, but
The clouds are merely swimming.

Still in one corner of the unknown,
Standing around boilingly
The face that cannot leave.

Will carry it on my back to the afterlife
So small and humble me
How about leaving it in the spare place of the sky?

Ever fresh sky
What if even the years don't leave and are lingering there?
With a weary mind
What if it blames itself for the swaying of the branches?

기대期待

막대기로 휘저어 버린 기억 모퉁이에는
나와 나란히 걸어온 무게
물 먹은 살갗 밑으로
대면의 시작이
환하게 열리고 있었다.

먼 날이 벼랑으로
빛깔처럼 흔들리는 행로
멍한 가슴 채울 게 없는
먼동의 소릴 듣는다.

잊혀진 온기 챙겨주는
더벅머리 손목 잡고 논둑을 돌아
깊어지는 연유.

기다림의 선잠자리에
어깨가 가 닿으면
가슴 흥건히 맺혔다 지는
바람은
흙 범벅이 된다.

The expectation

In the corner of the memory that was stirred with a stick
The weight that had walked alongside me
Under the skin of the moisture
The beginning of facing
Opened radiantly.

The far day toward the cliff
The swaying path of life like color
The stunned mind of insatiable,
I listen to the sound of the dawning sky.

Caring the forgotten warmth,
Turning around the ridge with grabbing its wrist of bushy hair
The deepening motivation.

In the uneasy sleeping place of waiting
When shoulders reach
After forming watery on the chest, then falling
The wind,
Becomes mired with soil.

처음의 사잇길로 맴돌다
비켜 서면
뒷굽의 물집이 저린다.

Hovering over the first side road,

Stepping aside

The blister on the heel aches.

제2부 Part 2

이별의 뒤란에서 만남의 뜨락으로
From the Back of Farewell to the Garden of a Meeting

차창에 번지는 노을로
엽서 색깔을 칠해 봅니다.

마주앉아 바라보던 시간
비에 젖은 바람을 고릅니다.
- 「바람 엽서」 중에서

With the sunset spreading on the train window
I am coloring the postcard.

The time with sitting face to face
I am picking the rain-soaked wind.
- The part of 「A windy postcard」

꿈

나는 바람을 감춘다.
그대는 나 몰래 바람을 날린다.
나는 아무것도 모르고
그냥 창문을 연다.
그대가 날려버린
나의 바람은 어디로 가버리고
그림자로 가득 찬
빈 공간을
엿보는 것도 모르고 있었구나.

흩어지는 구름 하나를
이렇게 건네 주듯이
만남은 처음부터
잠 못이루는 밤을 잉태하는가.

나는
풍선 속 바람인가 보다.

The dream

I hide the wind.
You blow the wind without my awareness.
I don't know anything and
Just open the window.
What you've blown away,
My wind has gone somewhere
Fully filled with shadows
Peeping that empty space,
Didn't even know that.

One scattering cloud
Like handing out this
The meeting, from the beginning,
Is it pregnant with the sleepless night?

I am
Maybe the wind in the balloon.

이별 뒤

너의 동공에 내리는 노을.

어느 날 한 마리 새가 된
나는

잘린 언어만을 골라 토하며
들길을 간다.

After farewell

The falling sunset on the pupils of your eyes.

One day, become a bird
I am

Choosing only the language that was cut off and vomiting it,
Going on a field path.

만남으로

이 밤
내가 동화되어
그대 신음을 들어요.
허물을 서로 사랑하면서도
말 다 못 할 그 무엇이 있는 것처럼
서로를 나누어 가지는 모양으로
이렇게 어둠이 되어 가네요.
꿈의 허공에 매인 추억들
그대에게 새겨 주려고
이토록 내가 바람 타네요.
비록 우리는 지금
가진 것이 없어도
나누어 가질 수 있는
하나의 하늘을
이렇듯 가꾸고 다스리지 않는다.
이 밤에
우리는 무엇이 될까나.
바람은 바람끼리
노을은 노을끼리
이웃하듯이

With a meeting

This night

I am assimilated,

Hearing your groans.

Loving each other's faults but

Pretending to have something remaining to speak

With a shape of sharing each other,

Becoming darkness like this.

Memories hung on the air of a dream

For carving it and giving you,

I am riding the wind like this.

Even though we are now,

Have nothing but

Can share

The only one sky,

Decorate it and don't control it.

This night

What would we be?

The winds are among themselves

The sunsets are among themselves,

Become neighbors

눈부신 꽃밭으로
충만한 것을 깊이 감추듯
하늘에 가 닿는
이 포근한 시간을
어떻게 건네 줄꺼나
어떻게 신음할거나.

Dazzling as a flower field,

Seems to hide deeply the fullness

Going and reaching to the sky,

This cozy time

How can I hand out?

How can I groan?

바람 엽서

차창에 번지는 노을로
엽서 색깔을 칠해 봅니다.

마주앉아 바라보던 시간
비에 젖은 바람을 고릅니다.

어디로 가는지 알 수 없이
간이역을 지나칩니다.

어둠에 번져오는 신호등 앞에서
무엇인가 파랗게 켰다가
무엇인가 빨갛게 껐다가
무엇인가 쥐어 봅니다.

돌에 눌린 누우런 숨소리로
어떻게 바람을 보듬어 봅니까.

오늘도 바람결에 나는
노을빛 엽서를 띄웁니다.

A windy postcard

With the sunset spreading on the train window
I am coloring the postcard.

The time with sitting face to face
I am picking the rain-soaked wind.

Without knowing where to go
I am passing through the way station.

In front of the traffic lights spreading in the dark
Something turned on bluely
Something turned off redly
I'm trying to grab something.

With the sound of yellow breath squashed by the stone
How do I hug the wind?

On the windy today again
I am posting a glowing postcard.

바람의 말 · 1

초록 하늘 아래서

눈감고 앉았노라면

바람이 더듬거리는 말

바람꽃의 말은 무엇일까.

A word of the winds · 1

Under the green sky

Sitting with my eyes closed

The stuttering words of wind

What's the word of windy flower?

진달래꽃

사르지 못할 것들은
모두가 다 아픔이렷다.

입김 번진 거울 속
한올한올 떠오르는 걸 빗어내리면
그 빛깔의 그늘 밑으로
푸름의 이끼가 돋는다.

지금도 벼랑 끝 안개
잡힐 듯 거기 서 있것다.

가까스로 손길 더듬어
아득한 하늘을 헤아려 본다.

노을빛 촘촘히 매달렸다
살 냄새 꽃그늘에 넘친다.

An Azalea Flower

The impossible things to burn,
All have been in pain.

In the mirror where the breaths are scattered
If combing out the rising thing strand by strand
Under the shadow of that color
The blue moss sprouts.

Even now the fog at the end of the cliff,
Might be standing there as if it could be grasped.

Barely groping with hands and
Guessing the infinite sky.

The glow of sunset hung densely
The smell of fresh overflows in the flower shadow.

저 혼자 피었을까
숨긴 것이 있다면
불길을 돌려놓고
잎새로 피워냄이라
시선 닿는 곳에
하늘로 오르는 모습이다.

Would it bloom alone?

If there's something hidden

Turning the flames back,

Because It's the blooming with leaves

Where the gaze reaches

It's the forming of soaring to the sky.

외 출

하늘이 바람에
잔물진다.

보드라운 풀꽃들이
비슷이 그림자에 기댄다.

구름이 히죽거린다
하늘 깃 옷고름을 펄럭이는
기상예보…….

Going out

The sky is quietly dyed
By the winds.

The soft grass flowers,
Obliquely lean on shadows.

The clouds are grinning
Fluttering with the string on the collar of the sky,
Weather forecast…….

섬을 떠나는 바다

바다는
달빛으로 표류하기도 한다.

섬을 떠나는 뱃전에서
물안개로 흔들린다.

아직도 저 파도는
바다의 꿈을 혼돈하는가.

포구에 밀려와 푸들대는 달빛
하얗다가 초록으로 너울댄다.

The sea, leaving the island

The sea
Sometimes floats as the moonlight.

On the sides of a boat, leaving the island,
Shaking in the water mist.

Does that wave still,
Confuse the dream of the sea?

The shivering moonlight, which is pushed to the harbor,
Swirls with turning white to green.

여정에서

그때는 내 맘대로 살았을까
나를 어둠으로 몰아 넣어도
어둠으로 동화되지 못했다
나를 진단할 수도 없었고
꺾을 수가 없었다.

아침을 내려놓으면
세상 근심 다 놓은 듯
심취할 때가 있었다.

귀를 막고 살아온 세월
나무에 봄이 기어 오르면
바람결에도 놀라 깨어나
꽃씨 따라 떠돌며
한바탕 웃는 것이 좋았다.

모든 것을 챙겨 둘 일이다.
꽃그늘에 숨어 있는
아지랑이 발목을 잡아둘 일이다.

On the journey

At those times, did I live my life as my mind?
Even rushing myself in the dark
Nor assimilated me into the dark
Nor diagnosed me
Nor broken down me.

When putting down my morning
As if I release all the worldly worries,
There was a time to be fascinated.

The years I have covered my ears
When spring climbs a tree
I surprised and awakened even the winds,
Wandering along with the flower seeds,
Was happy to a gust of laugh.

Everything needs to be kept.
Hiding in the flower shade,
The ankle of haze needs to be held.

낯익은 세상을 하루씩 처단하면서도
나는 나를 포용해주지 못한다.

While punishing the familiar world day by day but
I cannot embrace myself.

바람의 침묵 · 3

바람이 눈발을 세차게 어둠 속으로 몰았다.
그리고 바람은 뛰었다.
새삼 거울 속의 사물들은
거기 그대로 머물러 있었다.
아무도 모르게 얼굴을 파묻고
안심했거나 굴복하였다.
겨드랑이에 끼워 녹이던
언 손목이며 가슴까지도
바람결에 마주 서서
사는 것 같지 않게 살게 되었다.

The silence of the wind · 3

The wind drove furiously flurries of snow into the darkness.
Then the wind ran.
The objects in the mirror are again,
There, remained as they are.
Buried their faces without anyone knowing,
Relieved or yielded.
Melted with inserting under the armpit,
Their frozen wrists and even chests,
Standing face to face with the wind,
Become to live, unlike normal living.

하늘은 적막을 더한다

나는 이제 모든 것을 버린다.
너에게 쏠리던 눈빛도 버리고
몇 번이고 마음을 주저앉혀도
알 수 없는 무엇으로 돌아온다.

흔적을 지우고
순박한 얼굴로 헐떡인다.
오고 가는 길손을 들여다 본다.

한 때 풍요롭고 여유만만했는데
우울한 날 뒤쳐진 그림자만
같은 길을 걷는 속절없음이다.

내 자유는 무엇일까.
구름 한 조각 배고
강물이 지껄이는 소리를 귀담아듣는다.

뇌리에 쏟아지는 적막이
몸져누워 하늘은 적막을 더한다.

The sky increases silence

Now I throw everything away.
Throw away my look which I had focused on you,
No matter how many times I sit my mind down,
Returns to something unknown.

Clearing traces,
Gasping with an innocent face.
Looking travelers who are going back and forth.

Once rich and easygoing but,
Only the shadow behind me on a depressing day,
It's futileness in walking on the same path.

What is my freedom?
Laying my head on a piece of cloud,
Listening to the sound of the river's chatting.

A flood of silence in my memory,
Lying down, the sky increases silence.

안 부 · 2
-친구 안이모에게

미아리 시절
그 꼬맹이와 아직도 히히덕거리나,
잘나빠진 시 공부한답시고
너울대던 나를 째려보던 그 미소
아직도 간직하고 있겠지.

함박 눈이 내리던 안양 양지동 골목길로
담배꽁초 빨며 누런 덧니를 내보이던
육십 일년 겨울 추위를 잊지는 않았겠지.

겨울 코트를 전당포에 잡혀
됫박 쌀 사 오던 날, 철길까지 마중나와
홑겹 잠바를 내 어깨에 걸쳐주던
인간은 지금도 버리지 않았겠지.

자네 말처럼 시란 별개 아닐세
이제사 문득 깨닫나 보네.

아득한 정경이 눈발로 날리네
헛되지 않은 우리 꿈의 날이여.

Best regards · 2
- To my friend Ahn Iee Mo

The days of Mia-Ri
With that kid, are you still giggling?
Pretending to study poetry distinguishingly
The smile that glared at me, as I was fluttering
You may still have it.

The alleyway in Yangji-dong, Anyang, where it was snowing heavily
Sucking on cigarette butts and showing off yellow teeth,
Haven't you forgotten the cold of that winter in the year 61?

Pawned my winter coat,
On the day I bought rice of a gourd bowl, came to meet me on the railroad
The one that puts the one-layer jacket over my shoulder
You might haven't deserted it yet.

As you say, poetry is nothing special
Now I suddenly realize it.

The distant landscape blows with snowflakes
It is a day of our dreams that is not in vain.

지난 봄날에

허허로히 산그늘 따라 내려와
철쭉 지고 난 자리에 새로 태어난다.
손깍지 끼고 누워서
아직도 남은 사연
버릴 것이 절반이다.

무엇으로 둔갑할까.
몹쓸 바람 들면
버릴 것은 버려야 한다.

시샘하는 바람 속에서
무릎을 꿇는다.

기진맥진한 하루가
부질없는 게 아니어야지.

멱살잡힌 바람이 비틀거리다가
골목에 깔린다.
이것저것 하나씩 버려가면서
사는 것을 익혀가지만.

Last spring

Hollowly come down along the mountain shade,
Newly born again in the place of royal azalea's falling.
Lying down with crossed fingers
Still the remaining story,
Half is to be thrown out.

What shall it turn into?
If the nasty wind is pervaded,
Anything to be discarded must be thrown away.

In a jealous wind
I kneel down.

An exhausting day
It shouldn't be worthless.

The wind that was seized by the collar was staggering,
Laid in an alley.
I'm throwing away this and that one by one
I'm getting used to living.

너를 맞아 보낸다

그림을 그리다가 그 안에
빈 손으로 들어가 전생의 햇살을 줍는다

여기는 어디인가
길을 질러와서 기억할 수 없다

비 오는 엽서에는 떠다니는 구름과
들꽃이 가득 피어 있을 뿐이다

예감의 발길로 어디쯤 가다가
낯익은 찻집에 들르면
너의 모습이 보일까

아슴한 잠결 속에
팔을 괸 나는
다시는 찾아오지 않을지 모를
너를 맞아 보낸다.

Sending you after meeting you

While drawing, inside there,
Enter there with empty hands and picking up the sunshine of previous life

Where is here?
Can't remember the path because I came by a shortcut

In a rainy postcard
The floating clouds with field flowers are just full

Going somewhere with steps of foreboding,
Stopping by the familiar tea house,
Could I see your figure?

In the vague sleeping
Leaning on my elbow
Might never come again to find,
Sending you after meeting you.

꽃과 바람

마침내 그래도 나에게
돌아와 밟히는 기척
떠돌던 이야기는 이제
묻어두기로 다짐한다.

나름으로 가진 것 버려두고
아침으로부터 마주하는
바람의 얼굴.

하늘은 나에게
부끄러움을 알아차리게 한다.
꽃가지의 흔들림을
바람만의 손길이라 보지 말아라.

꽃과 바람은
한 하늘 가운데 내밀한 언어로
꿈을 이루게 하고
오늘과 내일을 짚어
향기로 피어나게 하는 섭리다.

A flower and the wind

Finally, however, to me
That signal returns, is trampled
The wandering story is now,
Determined to keep it buried.

Leaving what I have in my own way,
Facing it from the morning
The face of the wind.

The sky is to me
It makes me realize my shame.
The swaying of the flowery branch
Don't look at it like the touch of the wind only.

A flower and the wind
With an inner secret language in the midst of the same sky
Make achieve a dream,
Point out today and tomorrow and
It's the principle of blooming into fragrances.

제 3 부 Part 3

안부의 문턱에서 기도의 모서리로

From the Threshold of the Best Regards to the Corner of the Prayer

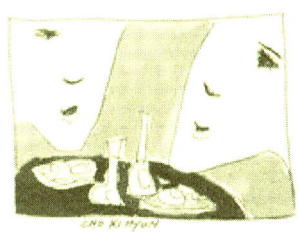

비 오는 산 너머
사라졌던 메아리가
되울릴 수 있다면
나도 또다시 돌아올지 모르지.
- 「소식을 마중하며」 중에서

Over the rainy mountain
The disappeared echo,
If it can resonate again
I could come back again.
- The part of 「Greeting the news」

당신의 일상 日常

때로는 남루하고
때로는 노을 같은
당신의 일상.

삶의 모든 정성이
채색된 마음 속
그늘진 곳에
나를 비끄러매어 놓고
팔랑개비로 돌고 돌아.

Your daily life

Sometimes, weary
Sometimes the sunset like
Your daily life.

All the sincerity of life
Inside a colored mind
In that shade
Tied me up
Spinning and spinning with a pinwheel.

기도에 대하여

그리움도 내색 않고

마냥 푸르른 하늘에
오직 몸짓으로 대답하는
전율.

About prayer

Without the showing of longing

To the just blueish sky
Answering only by a gesture
Trembling.

알 수 없는 마음

눈에 아무 것도 밟히지 않으나
그래도 무언가 떠돈다는 것은
가득 담겨
내게로 돌아오는 것.

한숨을 한 자락 깔고
뒹구는 바람이라.

모든 흔들림은
자기의 흔들림이 아니고
내 안을 휘도는 혼돈의 흔들림이다.

가로등 불빛이
안개 속에 묻힌 나를 찾아보지만
지난 일 헤집어
정녕 나를 잊고 지낸다.

Unknown mind

Nothing recollected on my eyes, but
Still, there's something about roaming
Fully filled,
Returning to me.

Spreading the piece of sighing,
It's rolling wind.

All the shaking is
Not the shaking of oneself but
The shaking of confusion with whirling in myself.

The streetlight
Finds me who is buried in the mist but
Digging up the bygones,
I am forgetting myself completely.

환幻

돌에 눌린 풀잎을 보면
세상은 온통 노랗다.

하늘도 땅도
보이지 않는 공간의 세계로
미끄러져 들면

삶은 온통 어지러움뿐이다
도대체 깨어날 수가 없다.

Unreality

Looking at the grass leaf pressed by a stone
The world is wholly yellow.

The sky and the ground also
Into the world of invisible space
If sliding in there

Life is all dizzy
I can't wake up earthly.

어떤 전율

산안개가 나를 감싸고 하늘로 오른다.
나뭇가지의 흔들림 속에서
햇빛이 흔들리고 있다.

밤낮없이 모든 것이
살아 있는 동안
내 작은 영혼의 흔들림은
어떤 전율이 되는가.

산은 말없이
나를 품어 준다.

이룰 수 없는 것
비망록에 거두어 담고서

온갖 시늉으로 지내가는 나는
벼랑으로 내달려 와
이름 없는 바람결이 된다.

Certain trembles

Mountain fog surrounds me, comes to the sky.
In the trembling of the branches
The sunshine is waving.

Everything all day and night
While alive
The trembling of my little soul,
What kind of trembling will it become?

The mountain is silent,
Embraces me.

The unattainable thing,
Gathering and holding in the memorandum and

Passing with all kinds of pretense
I rush into the cliff,
Become the nameless wind.

산 속에서

나뭇잎새 소리도
산울림이 되는가.

산울림은
산의 큰 자태가 된다.

산울림은
생각하지 않아도 좋았을
그 하늘이 산울림이다.

산울림이야 형체만으로도
몫을 다하는 거 아닌가.

죽음이야
누구라도 비껴갈 수 없는 길인데
누구라도 서러움 남기고 가는 길인데

함께 서 있는 나무에 안개로 다가와
어깨를 짚으며 남겨준 한 마디 말은
나더러 산울림이 되란다.

In the mountains

The sound of tree leaves also
Will it become mountain echo?

Mountain echo
Become the big shape of the mountain.

Mountain echo
Shouldn't have thought about it,
That sky is mountain echo.

Even just the figure of mountain echo
Doesn't it fulfill its portion?

The death is
Inevitable path to everyone,
The path with remaining with sorrow to everyone

Approaching with mist to the tree standing together
The only word that has left with touching on my shoulders is
Be mountain echo.

오늘도

너희들에게
아빠는 어떤 구름일까
바람 뒤곁에 서서
우두커니 서서
오늘을 바라본다.

너희들이 하루 걸러 입학하고
너희만한 중학생과 고등학생 옷매무새를
만지며 아침을 연다.

나는 술래가 되어 버렸다
아무것도 거역할 수 없는
무기력한 손아귀로
오늘을 비끄러맨다.

회오리 바람에 뒤엉킨
지푸라기처럼 맴돌다
제자리를 맴돌다가
스스로 분해되어 버린다.

Today again

To children
What kind of cloud is the father?
Standing behind the wind
Standing absently,
Looking at today.

You guys entered the school every other day and
The middle school and high school dresses that are the extent of yours
I adjust it and open the morning.

I became a tagger
Nothing to be disobeyed
With enervated grasp
I bind today.

The entangled by a whirlwind
Spinning around like straws
Spinning around in the same place,
I dismantle myself.

헌 책방에서

책장을 넘기다가
사랑의 푸른 시간과
공허했던 형상의 꽃잎을 본다.

그 어디에도 구속이 없는
밑줄 그어 번진
풀풀 냄새가
달콤한 영혼으로 뜬다.

머금었던 보랏빛 숨소리며
통통한 사랑의 그늘이며
아직도 물관이 숨쉬는 꽃잎.

소유가 바뀐 치맛자락이여
불면不眠의 낯선 허공을 휘감고
어디쯤 표류하는가.

깊은 밤
하늘 가득
남 몰래 한 움큼 쥐어지는
환상을 읽는다.

At the used book store

Turning the book page
The blue hour of love and
The flower petals of vain shape are seen.

Nowhere to be restrained
Spread by underlining,
The smell of grass water is
Floating with a sweet soul.

The purplish sound of breath with holding
The shade of chubby love
The flower petal that the vessel is still breathing.

The skirt whose owner is changed,
Surrounding the unfamiliar void of insomnia,
Whereabout is it drifting?

Deep night
Full of the sky
The thing that can grab a handful secretly
I am reading fantasy.

돌아보는 밀어

내 수중에 숨겨 지내는 것이 있다.
가을 햇살 자락에 날려오는
바스러진 날개의 나비이거나
그 거리에 남아 있는 것.
그 모습 그대로
눈물어린 채 멀어져간
내 유년의 꿈이다.

나는 언제나
눈보라 날리면 시린 입김으로
그 시절을 맴돌고 싶다.

누구의 심사이거나
밀려오는 마음갈피로
가까이 다가가 나를 붙든다.

부둥켜 안고 떠나보내지 말아야지
낯선 매무새로 서성이면서도
구겨지지 않게 고스란히 남겨 두어야지.

The secret word that is looking back

In my hand, there's a hidden thing.
Flown in by a piece of autumn sunshine,
The butterfly with crumbled wings or
The thing remained on that street.
The appearance as it is
The gone away with tears,
That's my juvenile dream.

I always
With a chilly breath when a blizzard blows,
Want to go around those times.

Anyone's mind or
With the border of mind that flows down
I closely approach and hold myself.

Will not send it with a big hug
Hanging around with the unfamiliar pearance of the dress,
Will leave it intact without wrinkled.

가을 문턱

장다리 대궁이
연보라 분을 바르고
봄날을 다 차지하더니

바람이 다가와
문지방에 앉으며
연지분 씻으라 하네.

세상 사는 것들은
파도로 출렁거리네.

가뭄이랑 태풍을
한 숨에 둘러 앉혔네.

아무래도 무엇인가
할 말이 남아 있나 보네.

꽃잎 속으로 잠적했다가
단물을 빨아올리는 햇살에
묻지 않아도 대답하고

하늘에 걸린 가을 낮달을
한 입 베어 무네.

The threshold of autumn

The stalk of flowers
Puts on lilac powder on its face,
Occupied the whole spring and

The wind comes and
Sitting at the threshold,
Asking it to wash the lilac powder.

The things that live in the world,
Is waving by waves.

Drought and typhoon
Were seated around at a burst.

Somehow something,
There may be left to say.

Vanished into the petals and
To the sunshine that sucks up the sweet water,
Answer it without asking and

With the moon on a day that hung in the sky,
Take a cutting bite.

밤의 정경

속내를 드러내는 것이 있다면
바위덩어리라고
어찌 숨쉬지 않겠는가.

잊을 수만 있다면
지난 일을 다 떠나보내야지.

마중할 것도 없는
허망의 껍질 벗어 놓고
남의 일인 듯
머얼기만한 촉수에 맞는 기색.

히끗대는 바람에 씻겨
나는 이 밤도
정지된 형상으로 각인되고 마는가.

The landscape of the night

If there's anything to reveal the intention
Even lump of a rock
How doesn't it breathe?

If I could forget it,
Should have sent out all the past.

There's nothing to meet it
Take off the vain skin,
As if it's other's business
The complexion that fits the just absent-minded tentacle.

Washed by glancing wind
This night again, I have
No choice but to be imprinted as a stopped figure.

그림자가 머무는 곳에

도금으로 빛나는 형상 앞에서
추한 나의 가슴 한 구석을 뒤집어 본다.

불꽃 속으로 기어들어가
형체를 알아볼 수 없이 녹아버리거나
아득한 지평에 서서 그대로 망부석이 되자.
서로 닿을 수 없는 손길로
마주 바라보고 날름거리는 혓바닥으로
어둠을 핥아 먹으며

세월이 머물다 떠나는 간이역사엔
사람보다 더 겁내고 흔들리는
그림자 하나 남는다.

Where the shadow stays

In front of the glittering shape by plating
I reverse the corner of my ugly mind.

Crawling into the flames,
Melted into an unnoticeable shape or
Let's stand on a distant horizon and intactly become a stone statue by waiting.
With untouchable touches each other
By seeing face to face with taking tongues in and out quickly
With licking the darkness

In the simple station where the years have stayed and left
More scared and trembling than human beings,
One shadow is left.

소식을 마중하며

어디로 가서
들꽃의 근성으로 피어나

생각이 열리어 오는 오늘
꽃잎을 한 잎씩 뜯으면서
손바닥에 나를 앉힌다.

무언의 손길로 등불을 켤 때
바람결 나의 온기여.

비 오는 산 너머
사라졌던 메아리가
되울릴 수 있다면
나도 또다시 돌아올지 모르지.

발길에 여울지는 것
온통 그을린 눈으로 뒤덮어 놓은 분수일 따름
삭아가는 내부를 안으로만 저울질하며
무언가 되돌리는 깊이로
항시 마중나갔지.

Greeting the news

Go somewhere and
Blooms into the patience of wild flowers and

Today when the thought is opened and coming
Tearing petals one by one,
Putting me on my palm.

When turning on the lamp with a silent touch
It's my warmth with the wind.

Over the rainy mountain
The disappeared echo,
If it can resonate again
I could come back again.

The abundant thing under my footstep,
It's only my limitation covered with wholly scorched eyes
Weighing only internally the decaying inside,
At the depth of something's return
Always I've gone out to greet it.

초록의 얇은 파문은
어지러움 속으로 다가온다.

청명한 밤
헐리지 않게 받쳐들으면
잊혀진 내가 돌아와 줄지 모르지.

A greenish thinned ripple,

Comes closer dizziness.

The clear night,

If supporting it up not to be broken down,

Maybe I'll come back after I've forgotten.

그믐밤에

별들이 깨어 있는 밤의 이야길
남의 일같이 되뇌다가
나를 마주한다.

지난 일은 모두가
건너고 피해온 자리

이런 참엔
스스로의 깊이를 헤아리고
밝혀볼 일 뿐이다.

이 밤
나는 혼자서 바람 날개를 접고
어둠을 벗어나와
새아침을 기다린다.

On the last night of a lunar month

The night story when the stars are awake
Repeating it like someone else's work and
I face me.

All the past things are,
The place that has been crossed and escaped

In this time
Reflecting my own depth and
I just enlighten it.

This night
Folding the wind wings by myself and
Coming out of the dark,
I wait for the new morning.

제4부 Part 4

기다림의 반석에는 사랑의 되새김이
On the Foundation of Waiting, the Reflection of Love is

무엇으로 둔갑할까.
몹쓸 바람 들면
버릴 것은 버려야 한다.

시샘하는 바람 속에서
무릎을 꿇는다.
- 「지난 봄날에」 중에서

What shall it turn into?
If the nasty wind is pervaded,
Anything to be discarded must be thrown away.

In a jealous wind
I kneel down.
- The Part of 「Last spring」

답신答信

도무지 알 수 없이
정지해버린 시간 속
어둠으로 가까이 다가가
한숨 죽여 바라본다.

세상은 나름대로 엿볼 수 있어도
내 빗댈 방도가 없어
산다는 건 참으로 영악해.

언제나 비롯됨은 미완이라며
마지막을 두고 창궐하던
친구여.

한갓 바람이야, 한 때의 설레임으로
지나가면 그만이겠지.

사람들은 서로 엇비슷이
오늘을 비껴가지만
친구여,
산자락에 걸린 구름 한 조각
어떻게 짚어 볼 수도 없구나.

A reply

Entirely unknowing
In the stopped time
Approaching into the dark,
I look at it with holding one breath.

Even though peeping the world in my own way
There's no method that I allude to and
Living is so clever.

Said always that the beginning has been incomplete,
Diffused after remaining the last
Dear friend.

Merely the wind, with the one-time thrill
If passing by, it's enough.

People are alike one another,
Evading today, but
Dear friend,
A piece of cloud hanging on the mountain edge
I can't even touch my hands on it.

바람이었지

꽃을 들여다본다.

꽃심에 발길을 멈춘 바람
연분홍꽃잎으로 스며든다.
땀방울이 어려 있다.

바람이 꽃잎에 휩싸여
어찌 너를
쥐락펴락 하랴.
그도 순박한 얼굴로 헐떡인다.

바람은 머무름이나 망설임이 없지만
유독 꽃심에 홀리는 것은
또 어떤 바람의 손짓 때문일까.

서로 모르게 흔적을 덮어주는 바람
그도 바람이었지.

It was a wind

Looks at the flowers.

The wind has stopped its foot at the center of the flower,
Permeates into the petals of pale pink.
The beads of sweat are flickered.

The wind is engulfed by the petal
How dare I,
Control you in my hands?
He also is grasping his breath with a naive face.

However, the wind has no stay or hesitation
To be possessed by only the center of the flower,
What kind of wind's gesture might it cause?

The wind that covers the traces unknowingly each other
He was also the wind.

정 적

외딴 집 마당에 피어난 앵두꽃.

보아주는 이 없어

먼 산 그림자가 다가와 논다.

작은 것 가운데

큰 것이 숨어 있어

빈 자리가 드넓다.

Stillness

Cherry blossoms in the yard of an isolated house.

There's no one to see it

The shadow of a distant mountain comes and plays.

In the middle of the small

The big one is hiding

The spare place is spacious.

가 뭄

풀잎은,

허수아비 숨소리를 엿듣다가

물을 빨아들이는 꿈결에

자지러지게 눕는다.

The drought

The grass leaves,

Eavesdrop the scarecrow's breath and

By a dreamy state of sucking waters

Frightenedly lie down.

그림자의 흔적

가을 모퉁이에 앉아
떠나는 모습을 지운다.

잰발로 나뒹구는 거리에서
까치발로 넘보는 하늘
잎새들이 손을 휘젓다가
구름 속으로 잦아든다.

어둠은 그림자를 밟고
나를 일깨운다.

살아온 것들을 가지런히 챙겨놓고
한쪽만 바라보고 살았음을 탓하랴만
성한 것은 성한 대로
사랑을 움트게 하는 씻김이다.

나는 너에게로 휘어지는 나뭇가지다.

The trace of a shadow

Sitting in the corner of autumn,
I erase the appearance of leaving.

In the street of trembling all about with swift foot
The sky that is coveted by tiptoe gait
The leaves are swinging their hands and
Slipping away into the clouds.

Darkness steps on the shadow,
Wakes me up.

Keep the things I have lived in order and
I won't blame my living for seeing only one side
What is good is as good,
That's the washing for sprouting love.

I am the tree branch that bends to you.

안면도 할매섬

차창에 어른거리는 하늘이
안면도에 와서는 바다였다.

하늘이 없고 바다뿐인 섬에
바다가 겹쳐져
아, 속살이 참 곱구나 싶다.

- 아이 뭐혀
옆댕이로 와 봐 -

한 때 외도로 한 세월 보냈더냐.
늘그막에 썰물 따라와
어둠 짙은 밀물에 바지가랭이 젖은 채로
어정하게 서서
몇 천 년을 두고
무슨 말을 궁리할까.

뭇 사람들은
저 할배를 바라보고
무얼 다스리는지.

Grandma Island, Anmyeondo

The sky that is glimmering on the car window,
When it came to Anmyeondo, it was the sea.

On the island with no sky, but only the sea
The sea is folded
Ah, the inner skin looks so pretty.

- Ah, what are you doing?
Come to the side -

One time, did you spend time on the affair?
Following the ebb tide in your old age
Wetting pants crotch by flood tide with deep dark
Awkwardly standing,
Remaining thousands of years
What kind of words are you mulling over?

Many people
Look at that grandpa and
What do they control?

빗속의 밤차

비 내리는 간이역에서
밤차를 보냅니다.

남기는 기적소리
다시금 기다림으로 번져옵니다.

눈을 감으면 그대로
깊은 잠에 빠질 것 같습니다.

꿈속에선 오래도록
강기슭을 거닐겠네요.

밤은 깊고
손길을 한없이 휘저을 뿐입니다.

The night train in the rain

At the rainy simple station
I let the night train pass by.

The remained sound of whistle is
Spreading over again as a waiting.

When closing my eyes, as it is
I feel like falling into a deep sleep.

For a long time in the dream
I'm going to walk along the riverside.

The night is bottomless and
Just stirring hands endlessly.

너와 나는

만남이었다
시골 장터의 풍물같지도 않았고
미사 때 울었던 아이도 없었다.

너도 나도
만남이 서툴러
나와 나는 그냥 우리가 되었다.

뱃고동소리에 부서지는 파도를
달빛에 담아

사랑으로
아픔으로
꿈으로
우리를 결박했다.

You and I

It was an encounter,
Not like the fairground of a country market
The child that cried during Mass also was not there.

You and I, too
Were clumsy at encounter so
You and I just have become us.

The breaking waves by the sound of the boat horn,
Holding it in the moonlight and

With love
With pain
With a dream
Have tied us up.

오늘도 나는

멀리 시선을 놓고
정녕 전생을 숨바꼭질 한다.

죽은 사람을 보면서 내가 산다.
가지면 무엇을 얼마나 갖겠는가.

누가 나를 배반하는가.
결국은 내가 배반할 것이다.

각기들 주인이라고들 하는데
염색체까지 오염되어
빛나지 않는 것.
내 자리가 아니기 때문일까.

내가 갖고 있는 것을
조금씩 시원히 잘라내면서 지낸다.

Today I also

Putting my glance afar,
I really play hide and seek of my past life.

I live by looking at the deceased.
If I have something, how could and what could I have it?

Who will betray me?
In the end, I will betray.

Each of them is said to be the owner but
Even chromosomes are contaminated
The beamless thing.
Is it because it's not my place?

What I've got,
I'm staying with cutting it freely little by little.

숲 속의 가로등

눈을 감고 있는 것은
잎새일까
가로등일까.

잎새에 가로등이 앉았다.
밤이 깊어서일까
그 무슨 속내를 헤매다가
잠들었을까.

잎새에 스치는 바람을 본다.
비에 씻긴 음성이다.

햇살은 하얀 구름 사이로
쏟아져 나와 창에 쓸어앉는다.

The street lamp in the forest

The one with closing eyes
Is it a leaf?
Is it a street lamp?

The street lamp sat on the leaves.
Maybe is it because of the deep night?
What inner feelings did it wander through and
Fall asleep?

Looking the winds brushing against the leaves.
It's a voice washed by the rain.

Among the white clouds, the sunshine is
Pouring out, sitting with sweeping on the window.

그대 사는 것

지새워 사위어도 남아 있는 것.

빈 말이 달게달게 익어 있는 것.

내디디면 허망의 바람 같은 것.

뜻 모를 내 안에서 그대 사는 것.

What you live

What it remains even after burning up all night.

What the empty word ripens sweetly and honeyedly.

What it's like the wind of vanity if stepping.

What you live within me without knowing its meaning.

헛소리 중에서

참으로 어리석은 나는
헛소리에 날려 어디쯤 가고 있는지 모르오.

처음부터 이제까지도
변하지 않은 것이 무슨 속내란 말이오.

잊혀졌다가 다시 떠오르는 모습이
얼마나 소용돌이치는지 누가 알랴만
애타고 속 타는 게 어디 이 뿐이겠소.

한껏 내달려 온 길
하염없이 바라볼 때가
얼마나 많아졌는지 모르오.

무엇이든 마음에 묻어 두지 마시고
헛소리로 날려요.

모든 것 다 놓아주고
떠난 그 자리에
남아 있을 자유여.

Among nonsense

So silly, I
Do not know where I am going to because of being blown by nonsense.

Even from the beginning to now
What's the hidden meaning that hasn't changed?

The image of being forgotten, then rising again to mind
Who knows how much it swirls?
It's not the only thing that is nervous and irritated.

The way where I have run as much as I can
The time when I look back it endlessly
I don't know how many are.

Don't hold it in mind whatever it is,
Blow it away as nonsense.

Let it release everything
The place where it left,
Will remain, it's freedom.

지금 나는

적막 깊이에서 나는 분해된다.
뒤엉킨 사념이 심장을 고정시켜 버린다.
나팔꽃이 해바라기 대궁을 향해
허공으로 손을 휘젓고 있는데
밤이슬 걸어 나오는 플루트소리
잊고 지낸 동안에도
먼동은 글쎄 한 다발로 피었다.

나의 일상은 항상
오기로 땅바닥을 뒹굴던 꿈이었다.

앞은 한 치도 볼 수 없어도
뒤돌아 보면 또렷한 추억들이
햇빛 속에 반짝이는
사금파리에 담겨져
나는 감동의 줄기를 뻗는다.

Now I am

Decomposed at the depth of silence.

The various entangled thoughts have fixed my heart.

A morning-glory towards the stalks of sunflower,

Is shaking its hands in the air and

The sound of the flute that walks through the night with dew

Even while I've forgotten it

The distant dawn indeed bloomed with a bundle.

My daily life is always,

It was the dream that is rolling on the ground with obstinacy.

Even though I can't see one inch ahead of me

Looking back, clear memories are

Twinkling in the sunlight,

Held in the porcelain chips

I stretch out the stem of heart touching.

자정이 넘으면
한 시절 시기에 뽐내던 거짓이
나를 노린다.
나는 자지러지지 않는다.
무지개로 태어나지 않으려 해도
심장을 드러낸 텅 빈 공간 속에
나는 어디에도 없다.
나는 하늘 뒤에 숨어서 앓는다.

After midnight

The lie that used to boast in its time,

It aims at me.

I will not be frightened.

Even though I don't want to be born as a rainbow

In the hollow space that exposed its heart

I am nowhere.

I'm ill from hiding behind the sky.

오늘 그리고 내일

아무리 살아도 알 수가 없다.
저승 가까이 쏘다니며
산다는 거
그게 어디 쉬운 일인가.

여름내 바람 뒤채이며
대궁에 매달려 죽음을 부추긴다.
아우성 가득 담긴 함정 속에서마다
앞 못 보고 사는 어제 오늘이어도
문을 열어 나를 가두고 싶다.

하늘이 낮아지고 있다.
성한 사람 죽은 시늉이라도
혼을 되찾을 수 있을 것 같기 때문이다.

귓속엔 호박잎새에 구르는 빗방울들
숨차게 몰아가는 숨결, 몸짓
그 뒷모습에서
누군가의 부름이 나를 바장이게 한다.

Today and tomorrow

No matter how much I live, I cannot know it.
Going about near the afterlife and
Living is,
That's not easy.

Struggled by the wind all the summer,
Encouraging death that is hanging from a flower stalk
In every trap where is filled by clamors
Even yesterday and today living with blind eyes,
I want to trap myself to open its door.

The sky is lowered.
Even the pretense of death from a healthy man,
Because it seems that I can regain my soul.

The rolling raindrops by pumpkin leaf in my ear
The rushing of breath, gesture
The shape behind
Someone's calling makes me hesitate.

무언가 맞으려 기다리고 있다.
만나고 헤어지면서
분명히 나대로 다스리는 세월
마련된 몫이다.

I'm waiting for meeting something.
Meet and break up so,
The years that are definitely controlled by my own way
That's a prepared share.

채색된 여운으로

세상에서 가장 깨끗한 과일
속살이

제 색깔로 숨겨져

정맥 속으로 아련히 퍼져가는
여운.

As a lingering imagery

The cleanest fruit in the world
The inner skin is

Hidden in its own color

Dispersing faintly into the veins,
Lingering imagery.

鄭松田 시인

- 1962년 「시와 시론」으로 등단.
- 서라벌예술대학 문예창작과 졸.
- 중앙대학교 국문과 및 동 대학원 졸.
- 용인시 죽전중학교 교장, 한라대학교, 경기대학교 겸임교수 역임.
- 세계시문학회 회장 역임.
- 한국자유시인협회 본상, 세계시문학상 대상, 경기도문학상 대상, 경기예술 대상, 현대 시인상 수상.
- 한국현대시인협회 지도위원, 한국작가협회 최고위원.
- 한국현대시인협회, 세계시문학회, 미당 시맥회 회원.

- **시집**
  「그리움의 무게」, 「바람의 침묵」, 「꽃과 바람」,
  「빛의 울림을 그린다」, 「내 이렇게 살다가」, 「바람의 말」.

- **자작시 감상 선집**
  「그리움과 사랑의 되풀이」, 「자연과 우주의 너울」,
  「내 삶의 소용돌이」, 「내 인생의 뒤안길」.

- **한영시집**
  「숨은 꽃」, 「너를 맞아 보낸다」, 「꽃과 아내」,
  「너와의 걸음걸이」

Poet Song-jun Jung

- Debuted with 「Poems and Poetics」 in 1962
- Graduated Literary Creation from Seorabeol University of Arts
- Received and graduated master's degree from Joong-ang University
- School president of Jukjeon Middle School in Yong-in City. Served as affiliated professor of Hanla University and Kyeongki University
- Served as the president of Literary Society of the World Poetry
- Awardee of Korea Free Poet Association, first line up at World Poetry Literature Award, first line up at Kyeonggido Literature Award, first line up at Kyeonggi Art Award, the receipient of the Modern Poet Award.
- Direction committee of Korea Modern Poet Association, the executive committee of Korea Author Association
- Member of Korea Modern Poset Association, World Poet Literary Society, and Midang Poet Line Association

■ Collections of Poems
　　「The weight of longing」, 「The silence of the wind」, 「Flower and wind」, 「Drawing the echo of lights」, 「Iliving in such way」, 「The words of the wind」.

■ Collection of poems for appreciation
　　「Repetition of longing and love」, 「The swell of nature and universe」, 「Whirlpool of my life」, 「Backwaters of my life」.

■ Korean-English Poems
　　「The hidden flower」, 「Sending you after meeting you」, 「Flowers and my wife」, 「Walking with you」

정송전 한영시집 2
너를 맞아 보낸다

2022년 8월 18일 1판 1쇄 인쇄
2022년 8월 22일 1판 1쇄 발행

지은이 | 정송전
펴낸이 | 김효열

펴낸곳 | **을지출판공사**

등록번호 | 1985년 2월 14일 제2-741호
주　　소 | 서울시 마포구 양화진길 41, 603호
우편번호 | 04083
대표전화 | 02) 334-4050
팩시밀리 | 02) 334-4010
전자우편 | ejp4050@hanmail.net

값 12,000원

ISBN 978-89-7566-215-7　　　03810

Korean-English Poems Collection of Jeong Song Jeon 2

Sending you after meeting you

1st edition printed August 18, 2022
1st edition published August 22, 2022

Author   Jeong Song Jeon
Publisher   Kim Hyo Yeol

Published   EulJi Publishing Company

Registration 1985. 2. 14   No. 2-741
Address 603. 41, Yanghwajin-gil, Mapo-go, Seoul, Korea
Phone 02-334-4050   Fax 02-334-4010
e-mail ejp4050@hanmail.net

Value 12,000 won

ISBN 978-89-7566-215-7   03810